God-Sized Hole

Living in God's Will or Your Own

Benjamin M. Carter Jr.

ISBN 978-1-0980-9641-0 (paperback)
ISBN 978-1-0980-9642-7 (digital)

Christian Faith Publishing, Inc.
832 Park Avenue
Meadville, PA 16335
www.christianfaithpublishing.com

Printed in the United States of America

To my amazing wife and our family and every friend along the way who has helped me. Without your support and sacrifice, this would not be possible. Thank you for dealing with the man who is me and understanding that I yearn to better serve you and the Lord through the daily refinement of my character. Obviously, this is a work in progress as you have seen.

Introduction

I never once dreamed of writing a book. Frankly I dread writing papers, so this is an interesting place to be faced with God putting this on my heart. In this book, I will be sharing the experiences I had coming to know the Lord Jesus Christ. The experiences however will be more along the lines of realizations the Holy Spirit has helped me to realize about myself. I have tried life two ways. The first way was living my own will, and the second, just several years old at this point, is living God's will the best that I can. I have come to recognize very plainly that when I am living in God's will, life moves as it should. I pray for reasonable happiness, and I am content. I find life to be filled with God's amazing grace, and I am free. However, there is also the pestering of the devil in my life. He had many years at the till of my existence while I was in the throes of active alcoholism, addictions, and full-out spiritual unhappiness and emptiness. Happiness in those days would be either so artificial that it never really felt right or so induced that it was destined to collapse at any moment.

So what happened? What was it like? And where am I now? Well, that will be the purpose of this book. It will focus on the journey that humans have gone through on this earth, but it will also show parallels to personal experience when applicable that I myself have gone through. I will not go into much detail of my own experience so that we may remain focused on what I believe God is trying to say from it; this is not an autobiography, and due to important factors of respecting people, there are also levels of detail that will not be disclosed.

Here is a little about myself. In the summer of 2013, I was accused of rape. In the summer of 2020, I live happily with my amazing wife, Elizabeth; my little boy, Benjamin (two years old); and my daughter, Mary Beth Marie (nine months old). I got sober by the grace of God and the program of recovery that I keep on January 4, 2016. God has had my life on the most amazing rocket ship I could never have imagined seven years ago. I am currently studying for my MDIV at Southwestern Baptist Theological Seminary as an online student while selling land to provide for the family God had given me. I was baptized the day before Elizabeth and I married on May 5, 2017. That day, I truly accepted Jesus Christ as my Lord and Savior, that He was born of this earth, suffered, and died for our sins and that Jesus is the Son of God and is Himself God.

This journey of filling a God-sized hole started with trying to fill it with alcohol, drugs, sexual relationships, perceived power/popularity, travel, fast living, etc. And this list was mine, so yours will have its own temptations and afflictions that are personal and perfectly fitted for the devil to use to keep you in darkness (John 8:12). God has a purpose for our lives that is well beyond and better than our own. If we are living in God's path, we are ultimately being the best versions of ourselves that He created us to be. The attribute of that is happiness and wholeness, unlike anything our best efforts could ever create or obtain by self-propulsion and desire. The goal is finding and maintaining our true character that God intended for us to have, continuously being shaped by His loving hands (Isaiah 64:8)

People say God doesn't speak anymore or perform miracles in the modern day. I hope my honesty and story serve as a burning bush (Exodus 3:3) for you. It is a miracle what God has done for me, where He has brought me from, what He has brought me through, and how I live and love life today. This is not a book about a man's perseverance, strength, or a comeback tale. This is a book about gaining everything through brokenness and surrender to God's will. It continues to be a daily process for me, but the challenges are much more bite-sized and of a daily variety as opposed to what they used to be.

Chapter 1

In the Beginning

God created man in His own image,
in image of God He created him; male
and female He created them.

—Genesis 1:27 (NASB)

God created man in His own image. To many, that means that God made us to look like Him, but I also think that He intended for us to act like Him as much as humanly possible. What does that look like? Well, the best example would be Jesus Christ. His whole purpose was to do God's will while on earth before ascending to heaven to rule with the Father (John 6:38). Jesus did however live a sinless life, and God never expected us to do that once we lost our sinless nature in the garden. From that day forward, we lived in a fallen state, separated from God.

God created man to be sinless, but humans quickly faltered in that. You may ask how this happened if God created us and is perfect. Well, the explanation in my opinion can best be explained by the very nature of God. He created us to worship Him and have fellowship with Him, but in His perfect love, He also gave us free choice to worship Him or not. God's ways are not our own (Isaiah 55:7–8), and something on the universal plane makes sense for God to give us free will. The easiest answer is because He didn't want us to be like robots, while the more complex answer is that for some reason, evil is allowed to exist in this universe, even when God has the power over everything and will ultimately destroy the evil. It is hard for our brains to comprehend the answer to this, and this leads us back to Adam and Eve in the garden.

God warned Adam not to eat of the tree of knowledge of good and evil.

> Then the Lord God took man and put Him into the garden of Eden to cultivate it and keep it. The Lord God commanded the man saying, "From any tree of the garden you may eat freely; but from the tree of the knowledge of good and evil you shall not eat, for in the day that you eat from it you will surely die." (Genesis 2:15–17 NASB)

Adam listened to God at first, but with Eve, things got complicated. There were two humans. They began to influence each other's thinking, and the devil seized in on an opportunity. He told Eve a lie (Genesis 3:5), that God was keeping from her something amazing out of His desire to control them. Yes, God was keeping something from them, but not for the devil's stated reasons. God was trying to protect them from themselves. This "original sin," as it is so aptly called, led to the human race's first encounter with separation from God's will; and until the arrival of Jesus Christ, we were separated from God since in His perfection, anything outside of His will cannot be in His presence or it will be destroyed. Darkness cannot exist when there is light present in the same space, much like air and water do not mix but slightly different because light actually overtakes the darkness. So God cannot accept us into Himself when we are full of sin. In the Old Testament before the coming of Christ, the priest had to prepare themselves to enter a space in the tabernacle that was called the holy of holies. They would only enter this space at times that God identified, and there was a whole process of cleansing and sacrifice in order to enter this space; otherwise they would die (Leviticus 16:2–28 NASB).

God had created a perfect environment for Adam and Eve. He wanted them to enjoy it and also enjoy Him for creating it all. Unfortunately, though she had been warned, Eve was deceived by the devil to eat the fruit of the forbidden tree (Genesis 6:3). The Bible says after the serpent spoke to her, she looked at the tree differently, and it now appeared "good for food, delightful to the eyes, and desirable for wisdom." Again the fruit of the tree looked good, delightful, and desirable. How many men and women have fallen into the same traps today looking at the desires of the world? This was the beginning of our separation from God. The first humans caused this separation, and the human race has suffered for that sin until the day that Jesus came to bear it for us with His blood (Isaiah 53:6).

If we think about this for a moment, it conjures up a couple of questions such as the following: What is the point? Isn't it unfair that we always have to do what God says is right? At least these were the questions I had from my teenage years to my midtwenties. Coupled with mind-altering drugs and some study of philosophy in college, I was sure that I had a valid answer to all this. I agreed with the teachings from philosophers like Descartes and Paley that God existed, God created everything, yet God was more like a clockmaker who once He sends the clock off is not so much concerned with its actions and life. For me, however, I did believe that if He corrects that clock, it stops keeping time or altogether stops working. The problem I had with organized religion was this—the world didn't seem to be a fair place according to my understanding, and I seriously doubted that the Creator of everything cared about our day-to-day lives, much less us spending time every Sunday to worship Him. We will go into this further later in the book, but I share this to show how I can see that Adam and Eve wanted to gain more knowledge in the very beginning. Something in our very nature and free will makes us want to know more, gain more, and have more. It can be as simple as wanting more free time to the complexity of wanting to run the nation.

Each person has their own desires. God made us this way so that we could flourish naturally. It made perfect sense for a being that needs food, shelter, water, and procreation to have all these natural desires; but God never intended for us to use them for our own purposes and pleasure. I am not saying that God wants you to be boring and not enjoy your life, but just like Adam and Eve, He has provided everything for you to live a healthy life, and like them, we often choose to bend or break the rules for what we think is better. Also, like them, if we continue down this path to the point of sin, which is anything outside of God's will (I used to have a real issue with this word until I understood it better), God has no other choice but to correct our path. This sure feels like unfair punishment to us, but what I have come to find is it is our own personal brokenness that we have to endure. God gives us circumstances that are uncomfortable for us in order to help us grow more into the person that He intended us to be. As you will see in the chapters to follow, this can be a very painful process.

CHAPTER 2

God-Sized Hole

Organized religion seemed incredibly hypocritical to me. Every "religious" person that I met seemed uptight, rigid, boring, scared, nervous, and worst of all judgmental and full of hierarchy. I used to always quip, "Jesus followers are the fanatical children of overly strict parents. They just don't know how to have a good time." This was typically proven to me (or at least I thought) because when I would have parties and those friends of strict parents would drink, they looked like they had broken out of prison and often couldn't even handle it very long before they get sick or pass out. I now realize that simply with anyone who never had alcohol, it had absolutely nothing to do with the household or religion they came from. I also had a belief that everyone has their own personal relationship with God, and this belief was actually correct, but not the way I thought of it as I will expound on in chapter 6. I thought that since everyone has their own personal relationship with God, Christianity was too limited. I wouldn't have known the term then, but I believed in "universalism," meaning all will be saved as long as they pursue God (Hesselgrave 69). I truly thought all the world's religious people would make it to heaven as long as they sought God. Jesus was not the only way into heaven. Unfortunately for me, I had no idea what I was talking about, and the devil had no interest in letting me go easily. He was having too much fun causing one of God's children (and those around him for that matter) angst and unhappiness.

Those were definitely not the people that I wanted to be, much less listen to. I used to often say ignorant things like, "I'd like to believe God cares about how I live, but I have never met Him to ask Him and He has never reached out, but I think we should be nice and help others." I also thought that life was measured on your good versus your bad, and in the end, you would be judged for that before you entered heaven. Another part of me doubted that we even went to heaven and that when you died it was just over. Your carbon returns to the universe in time to do whatever it wants with it. Maybe we are even reincarnated. I thought at one psilocybin latent period of my life that it would be really cool to come back as a dolphin and spend my days swimming in the West Indies in the Caribbean Sea.

The problem was this—all these thoughts never lasted and never brought me peace. There was always something missing, and I knew it. So when in doubt, I would just go back to having fun. It wasn't all a bad time in my twenties. I really did have quite a good time! But the problem was growing underneath, and I was spiritually decaying from the inside out. I never could quite get enough of anything. I also searched for the next fun experience, and that was the real beginning of the period of my life trying to fill a "God-sized hole" with partying, travel, fun on the water, sexual relationships, lots of drinking, and lots of living life large and loud. They made me the social chairman of my fraternity two years running for good reason. I was successful at having a big party. Lots of everything to enjoy.

I want to take a quick trip forward in my life. I was thirty-one years old sitting in an early morning men's meeting for recovery while in rehab out in California. I had ended up in this rehab because I was terrified of the trouble that was rapidly appearing in my life. I was pretty much sure there was no happy future for me, but I hoped if I got sober, maybe I could survive to figure that out. As I sat in the back of this men's meeting above a bank in Pacific Palisades, California, a man started to share his story. I was listening as the trouble in his life got worse, and worse, and worse. Then he seemed to cheer up and say, "And it was then that I realized I had been trying to fill a God-sized hole." A flicker of a spark begun in my head that I could never have imagined at the time. That man didn't coin that phrase, and neither did I, but nothing in my life could be closer to the truth. At that point in my life, I had loneliness growing inside of me that assured me that I was very alone and apart from everyone else. This feeling had been in my life since childhood and would aspirate in different forms, at different ages. Around thirteen, I was diagnosed with prepubescent anxiety. I was having anxiety attacks that would sometimes go to the point of panic attacks. Then to justify the anxiety even more, I had several very scary episodes where I had what they now call a complex migraine. This was not like a regular migraine. It looked more like a stroke or seizure. I would lose control of one side of my body and slur my speech. It was incredibly scary, and they gave me a very powerful narcotic that I traveled around with just in case one came on. So in addition to already having a level of discomfort, I often feared I was going to get embarrassed by one of these episodes.

Jump forward some years, and now I am in high school. I had figured out by this point that I really enjoyed drinking and, in the late years of high school, smoking large amounts of pot. This time period was also where I really began looking at the world around me and how it worked. I think it is important to share that I was no atheist. I would say my prayers nightly and believed in God, but it was more like going through a shopping list when I prayed. There was no conversation taking place. By senior year of high school, I began to realize that I had grown out of a lot of social discomfort I felt, but not because it wasn't there. It was because I had started to treat it differently. I can remember many a time that I would be at a party and leave to go sit, drink, and smoke by myself, even more so if the party was at home. The real kicker would be when I rejoined the party, it felt like no one even noticed I had left most of the time.

In college, this grew into a propensity to find the people that liked to party as hard as I did, and out of the pigeonhole of who I was at the school I attended for fifteen years growing up, this also expanded to relationships with girls. I say all this to show what had begun to occur was I was truly beginning to have an identity that I felt I had control of, and I was beginning to take the idea of feeling like there was a missing part of myself that I needed to fill. At this point in my life, I was oblivious to the fact that I need God! As the college years continued, the partying became more intense and the substances more powerful. It was not uncommon in those days to be up all night and then take something to pass out and sleep until the early afternoon. On the weekends, we would just wash and repeat, usually getting on a boat or heading to the beach with a couple of pills and hair of the dog drinks to help us on our way.

As the years progressed, the hole became emptier, and I truly found myself being sold the biggest lie the devil tells us all—"If only you had _____, then you would be happy." I used to love lines and movies that I felt like understood my disconnection from the world around me, how they just didn't understand the huge heart I had, and how important caring for others was to me. I related with Bruce Wayne in *Batman Begins* when he (Christian Bale) saw the love of his life after making a ridiculous scene with two women swimming in the fountain of a restaurant in a hotel he owned. He tried to tell Rachel (Katie Holmes) that he really was much more on the inside. She looked at him soaked in a tux with two girls in robes behind him and said, "It's not who you are underneath, but what you do that defines you." Later in the movie, Batman (Christian Bale), now in all of his amazing selfless sacrificial heroism, said the same line back to Rachel, proving that what she said was true and he deserved to be believed. Here is the problem with this wonderful paradox. It leaves out a very true element of our nature—if we live with a different person on the inside from who we present to the world, then it is impossible for us to have a fulfilled life. Of course, people are going to have elements of their self that they don't openly share with others, but what I am talking about is this. I always felt like there was a side that I presented to people and then underneath how I really felt. Back to that statement the devil says, "If only you had _____, then you would be happy," I would fill that blank over and over again. Often I found that I was not able to keep what _____ was or if I did, losing enjoyment from it as the shine wore off over time, I was left again with myself and discontent.

This may seem fairly obvious to a healthy person, but I was far from healthy. I was a victim of the symptoms and not actually dealing with the underlying problem, though many a therapist had tried.

Going back to the example from the *Batman Begins* movie, there is another major flaw in thinking that what we do defines us. I can think back on many times in my life that I did something good for other people, got involved with a good cause, and gave monetarily to one and always realized one thing. The times that I was truly moved to give, I was very content, while the times that I gave with the expectation to receive something in return, I was not only let down but also resentful. I think a lot of us try so hard to present what we think the world wants to see to claim "they are so amazing, they are so kind, they are so great" that we lose track of the fact that unless we are a whole person, the works (though beneficial to others receiving them) are in vain as far as growing spiritually.

We are not defined by what we do, and we are made up of what we think, how we feel, what actions we take from it, and then how we respond to the outcome. To this day, incredibly unhealthy thoughts race through my mind, and sometimes they seem to come out of nowhere, while other times, it is much clearer. On some level, I am not getting what I want, and the devil seizes the opportunity to ask me that age-old question, with an adjusted twist, "Wouldn't it feel great if you had _____ again?" A friend in recovery said this, "We are responsible for our second thought and first action."

Being able to recognize these attacks of the flesh and taking it to Jesus is the first victory and the most important one to continue to grow as the man God intends for me to be. The crazy side effect of this is that in the middle of turmoil and discomfort, I can have utter peace and satisfaction as long as I am staying present with God and out of myself! It's not really a side effect, but it's how God made us and intended for us to be (Philippians 4:6–9).

CHAPTER 3

Solomon's Life

*Now God gave Solomon wisdom and very
great discernment and breadth of mind, like
the sand that is on the seashore. And Solomon
wisdom surpassed the wisdom of all the sons
of the east and all the wisdom of Egypt.*

—1 Kings 4:29–30

King Solomon was the son of King David, and as he was becoming King Solomon, he prayed for great wisdom and knowledge (2 Chronicles 1:10). God was so moved by his prayer and the fact that Solomon's request did not include asking for riches, wealth, or honor or the lives of those he hated (2 Chronicles 1:11), God not only granted Solomon's request but also said He would give him riches, wealth, and honor. Obviously, Solomon was very pleased with this at first, and he began to build a great temple to the Lord like no structure that had ever been seen at that time.

As God promised, He began to bless Solomon with riches and power, and at first all was well and as God intended. Solomon gained quite a name for himself and his wisdom was sought by many, and in came the queen of Sheba.

Solomon was flourishing, and his wisdom and knowledge had become renowned well beyond his lands. The queen of Sheba came to visit him to test his knowledge and to see firsthand the wealth and power Solomon had obtained. After testing Solomon, she admitted her utter amazement, and in her defense, she gave glory in the right direction, which was to God. The queen acknowledged how God had blessed Israel by giving them the wisest king. "Blessed be the Lord your God who delighted in you to set you on the throne of Israel; because the Lord Loved Israel forever, therefore He made you king, to do justice and righteousness" (1 Kings 10:9 NASB). Jesus also proclaimed that the queen of Sheba had a righteous path to seek the power of God. "The Queen of the South shall rise up with this generation at the judgement and shall condemn it, because she came from the ends of the earth to hear the wisdom of Solomon; behold something great that Solomon is here." (Matthew 12:42 NASB)

The story of Solomon quickly took a turn in the wrong direction after the experience he had with the queen of Sheba. Soon leaders of many nations came to seek his wisdom bearing gifts of gold, garments, weapons, spices, horses, and mules; and Solomon amassed 1,400 chariots and 12,000 horsemen (1 Kings 10:24–26). The train was leaving the station, and Solomon was turning away from God. Now many may ask, "But why did God let this go to excess? Shouldn't He have warned Solomon and didn't He tell him He was going to make him a king greater than any other?" Well, yes, He did tell him that, but He had also warned the kings of Israel of how they should and shouldn't live back in the book of Deuteronomy. Solomon was about to step all in what God said not to do. He took many wives, he amassed a large army, and he used his wisdom for his own gain, not God's. And finally at the depths of all this sin, Solomon began to worship the false gods of his many wives (seven hundred wives to be exact, how exhausting!).

In keeping with the theme of this book, what we are looking at here is a man of God's choosing who got off course and decided to try and replace God with all these earthly possessions and power. Solomon started on a righteous path, but now he was "running with the devil." Solomon's existence came due to an insatiable desire for power, possessions, sexual desire, and fame. Much like many of us today, this glamorized existence truly drove him mad, and we get to see how he feels about it all in the end after God sets this poor lost son straight. The culmination of all of Solomon's sin ultimately serves as his brokenness, and ultimately God uses it for good as we get to the book of Ecclesiastes and many of the Proverbs.

As Solomon reached an older age, he had compromised so much that he was worshipping false gods that his wives introduced to him. "For it came about when Solomon was old, his wives turned his heart away after other gods; and his heart was not wholly devoted to the Lord his God, as the heart of David his father had been" (1 Kings 11:4 NASB). Solomon was building temples and idols for these gods. To give an example of how far Solomon went down this rabbit hole, one of the false gods he was worshipping called Molech was a god whose followers would sacrifice young children by burning them. Needless to say, God was not happy with Solomon at this point and proclaimed to bring difficulties into his life (1 Kings 11:11).

Solomon had to suffer many hardships, but what I can most easily relate with was the work that was done on him by God through all his disobedience. Solomon in his later years had a return to the Lord and had finally realized that his attempts to pursue the desires of his flesh had brought him nothing but unhappiness and angst. After years of trying to gain all he could, he found himself completely drained and empty. He also viewed the pursuit of the desires of the world was not only foolish but also worthless.

The following is a paraphrased excerpt from Ecclesiastes chapter 2 (NASB):

> I explored with my mind how to stimulate my body with wine...I enlarged my works: I built houses for myself... I made gardens, ponds of water, bought male and female slaves, I possessed flocks and herds larger than all who preceded me... I collected silver and gold, and the treasure of kings and provinces, I provided myself many male and female singers, the pleasures of

men—many concubines. Then I became great
and increased more than all...all that my eyes
desired I did not refuse them. I did not withhold
my heart from any pleasure... Thus I considered
all my activities which my hands had done and
the labor which I had exerted, behold all was van-
ity [futile, worthless] and striving after the wind
and there was no profit under the sun.

I think it is obvious what God intends for us to learn through
the life of Solomon. The story of Solomon began with God wanting
to bless him and answering his prayer for wisdom. Unfortunately for
Solomon, much like Adam and Eve, his human condition took over,
and he began to use God's gifts for his own gain. At the end of his
life, Solomon made a plea that all should fear God and follow His
commandments and direction for their life (Ecclesiastes 12).

Solomon had great wisdom for modern men and women.
Solomon's pursuits for his own pleasures, riches, power, and fame
led him to compromise. At first, the compromises were small, but
once he started cutting corners, the compromises became bigger and
bigger until they grew to the point of the epitome of sin, which was
the worship of self and false gods. God warned Solomon along the
way as well, and I would like to believe that just like me, along the
way, he knew what he was doing was wrong in his heart. I can also
say however from personal experience that the devil is very good at
helping create enough noise and an insatiable spirit within us that we
truly can begin to believe that we must have something to be happy,
or worse yet we deserve to have things that God never intended for
us to have. Solomon liked the feeling of being admired. Solomon
liked the feeling of being powerful. Solomon liked the physical pleasures that his sexual relations brought him, but it was obviously never
enough for Solomon. Once he started to live a life outside of God's
will, he began to go more and more off course.

I think it is fair to assume that Solomon was much like the
young rock star or actress, loving all the attention, the newfound
fame, having everyone looking at him in awe, and becoming more

and more accustomed to extravagant living and possessions. The next party must be crazier, the next girl must be hotter, and the next vehicle bigger, brighter, and faster than the last. The cost of each of these things was also becoming greater and greater as well. When I say the cost, I am not talking about the ever-increasing price tag (but yes, that is true as well). I am talking about the cost to Solomon. Solomon had been given great wisdom and power to do God's will, but his will was rotting him from the inside out, and over time, it finally broke him.

Solomon writes, "In the day of prosperity be happy. But in the day of adversity, consider God has made the one as well as the other... Do not be excessively righteous, and do not be overly wise. Why should you ruin yourself?" (Ecclesiastes 7:14). Solomon also warns us of his spirit away from God. "It is not good to eat much honey, nor is it glory to search out one's own glory. Like a city this is broken into and without walls is a man who has no control over his spirit" (Proverbs 25:27–28). There are many examples that Solomon has left us with through his writings in Ecclesiastes and Proverbs that help us to understand the utter futility and despair we will experience living outside of God's will, living in sin. Not only is it easy to get ourselves focused on ourselves and our own gains, but also it is, unfortunately, a paramount part of our fallen fleshly nature while here on earth.

CHAPTER 4

The Bottom

I have lived a very fortunate life. I grew up in a loving family that provided for me the best life I can have as far as attention, luxurious travel, great adventures, and financial support to pursue business opportunities and dreams. Much, if not all, of that was an amazing blessing, but it did not fill a God-sized hole, and there is nothing my incredible parents can do to change that through all their generosities, love, and care. They gave me a great financial foundation and dare-to-dream attitude that led me to pursue developing restaurants as a franchisee that at first were quite lucrative. I used to own a helicopter. It was incredibly fun by all means, and I hope my days of flying one aren't over. (Trust me, it is even better than what you imagine flying one would be like. It's like a magic carpet ride that can also be a roller-coaster ride that you tell where to go.) There is also a real freedom being up in the air by yourself deciding where you want to go and what you want to see. But even with all that, I would often have a sinking feeling during or after when realizing that someday this too would likely not satisfy me, at least not the way it had. I wasn't even aware of the fact that I one day wouldn't even be able to afford to rent one, much less own one. What a joke the devil plays on us sometimes. We are so blind to the inevitable truth that is just around the corner. Don't get me wrong, I am not against nice things or luxurious living. I am however afraid of how it makes me feel, and it begins to define who I think I am. True worth in life is not preceded by a dollar figure, square footage, horsepower, or meters in length. It is what we have in our spiritual connection to God that provides us true worth. Jesus Himself said, "It is easier for a camel to go through the eye of a needle than for a rich man to enter the kingdom of God" (Mark 10:25 NASB). I don't think I need to clarify this, but Jesus meant this as a metaphor.

In the fall of 2013, I was living in Charleston, South Carolina, and enjoying several months of sobriety after a terrifying summer, and all seemed like it was going to be wonderful. Several months earlier, I had hit what I consider to be the beginning of my bottom, and it would take several years to come out of it. I had been arrested trying to buy drugs one night and then just several nights later set the stage for an allegation that would consume my life for several years to come. I was in my apartment working on the phone in Charleston when a knock came upon the door. I could tell that this was not a pleasant neighbor coming by to say hello. It had an urgency and force to it. I opened the door to probably five police officers who quickly grabbed me and took me in. After what seemed like an eternity, I was able to speak to an attorney who told me what I had been charged with, and I felt like I was in nightmare. It did not seem real. I am not going to go into any details as it is not appropriate or consequential to this book, but I can tell you that the next three years of my life until the case was dismissed was like living in hell. There was not one moment of rest, and it was completely terrifying. It also was far from a private matter as the newspaper took the mug shot from the drug arrest prior and attached it to a very detailed story about the allegation. It is a horrible existence to walk around fearing people and places because of the look people give you, the majority of which have either heard or made up whatever story is most horrible to them. The stress got so immense in time that I had a constant ringing in my ears, an inability to focus on anything, and at its peak I literally couldn't tell you what I had for lunch earlier that day come midafternoon. I was terrified and pushed through all this, hoping and praying that God was with me.

After surviving all this, I was completely destroyed, but there was more to come. I was in a relationship that made it through the whole terrifying period only to come to an abrupt end, and I was fighting very hard to stay sober. Life had gotten to a point that I truly didn't see a future. "Who will want to ever be in a relationship with me now?" "How was I supposed to function in a world that thought I was a monster, and how in the world do they expect me to stay sober through all of this?" Those were the questions that took turns attacking me between moments of obsessive despair playing back over the hurts of the last several years and all kinds of future tripping where it didn't ever get better. Life got to a point where all I did in a day for months on end was walk my dog around the block and go to recovery meetings. I spent hours sitting on the sofa trying to just nap the day away because I didn't want to have to deal with the reality I lived in. I felt like I lived in a fishbowl, and at this point, I truly only felt like isolating but yearned so dearly to not be alone all the time. I started reading books about recovering from trauma and spiritual growth books like *the Power of Now*. I couldn't sleep at night, and I would toss and turn with my thoughts. I felt like I was drowning in the sea with no land in sight. I wished that something would change, something would give me hope, and what happened next was definitely not what I expected.

I was on the way to see my mother for Mother's Day and had stopped at a gas station in the middle of nowhere of I-26 in South Carolina. My little "Labkin" (Labrador retriever and Boykin Spaniel mix) Buddy was with me, and I had let him out to run around while I filled up the tank. As usual, I was consumed with thoughts about my life, all that had happened, how alone I felt, and what in the world was next for me when I realized Buddy was over by a trash dumpster nosing through something. I called him back to me, loaded him up, and off we went to see my parents without another thought about it. A day and a half later, Buddy started acting very strange, and within a couple of hours, we were at the UGA animal hospital. By this point, Buddy was bleeding so profusely internally that it was coming out of his nose and mouth. Buddy had gotten into rat poison, likely from that gas station I guess, but we will never really know.

As Buddy's condition declined and they prepared him for an operation, I took off my shirt and wrapped him in it so he wouldn't feel like I left. At this point, I walked out of the building to my mother, who was waiting there for me. I remember hanging over her shoulders, shirtless, and bawling, crying, and saying to her, "If God takes this dog from me, I have nothing left." Well, I was 100 percent correct, but not in the way God intended it. I made a gut-wrenching decision to put Buddy down the next day. He was suffering immensely, and the prognoses was very bleak. That moment in my mind was the official fissure between my old life and the man that I am today. I had to lose everything I knew, and the process forward was very difficult, and at first there was no land in sight. However, God knew exactly where I was and exactly what was to follow. He was also right there and never left my side for an instant, but I wasn't aware of it yet. Some months earlier, I had started lying in bed at night asking God to reveal more of Himself to me. I had been doing this reluctantly but desperately because ever since I had been little, I had said my prayers and believed in God (other than some "self-enlightenment" seasons of life). The reason I was reluctant was because I was sure that God knew me as a liar. For many years, I would stay out all night partying, and often as I lay in bed fearing that I had gone too far, I would say to God, "God, please don't let me die. I promise I won't do this again. Just don't let me die." And I meant those prayers at the time, I really did, but unfortunately, I couldn't seem to keep the promise.

Some weeks or months would pass where I would reel things back, but ultimately my disease of alcoholism would creep back in, and a little voice would say to me, "Hey, you've been really good. Maybe we can party a little bit." "Hey, it wasn't really that bad. You're just going through a hard time." "Hey, we made a big business deal today. You deserve to celebrate." "You're not going to meet anyone sitting at home alone. You need to be social and that takes some drinks," and the list could continue. We alcoholics call this the cunning, baffling, and powerful element of alcoholism. I personally can tell you it's simpler than that. It's the devil (evil). He wants to keep us trapped and separated from God just like he did back in the garden of Eden and for all in existence since then. I often reflect on the darkest times in my life and thank Jesus that He was there even though I didn't truly realize it at the time.

As I sit here writing this book and telling you of my bottom, I can tell you that it is still bizarre to me that I am talking about my own life. Sometimes it is hard to believe that was even me that went through those circumstances and trials. The truth of the matter is this—it's not me that went through them. Yes, the same human did but not the man that I am today thanks be to God and His amazing grace. We all have our own afflictions that we have to deal with in life. You may be smack in the middle of yours right now. Until we are able to recognize them and willing to work through them, we are slave to them on some level. When this becomes apparent, our lives typically begin to fall apart, but the blessing in this is—we are now aware of them and can begin the process of awakening from the nightmare.

CHAPTER 5

The Enlightenment Era

Humans have questioned the existence of God since very early on in our creation. However, as humankind grew in education and study of ourselves and the world around us, we began to question things differently. The early societies usually had some concept of a god, much like if you were to reach an indigenous people groups these days that had no connection with the outside world, they would likely have their own belief system relative to natural order with a supreme being, made up of a god or multiple gods.

For the purposes of this book, I am more so focused on giving the current-day reader an understanding of where humans have questioned God in the past in relation to modern society and popular beliefs (or lack thereof) today. To give a better picture of how I think we as a Western culture came to our current ideas about God, I have chosen what I see as a major turning point in our history—the Enlightenment of the late seventeenth and eighteenth centuries. In the words of Britannica, "the Enlightenment was an intellectual movement...in which ideas concerning God, reason, nature, and humanity were synthesized into a worldview. Central to Enlightenment thoughts were the use and celebration of reason, the power by which humans understand the universe and improve their own condition."

As we advanced as a species to levels of higher intellectual thought, which birthed the sciences, philosophy, psychology, and modern medicine, we began to question more of the world around us in an ever-present hunt to find the truth to how things worked around and in us. This movement ultimately led to the rise of deism, which plainly states, "God exists, but God doesn't interact with the world or universe anymore." The very essence of the Enlightenment was the expansion of the importance of the individual and also to be skeptical of all we had been taught or previously conceived to be true. I think that it is only logical to assume this way of thinking would put us on a course away from God. In essence, God made us intelligent so that we could grow and learn, but He did not intend for us to seek our own superiority or self-worship through knowledge. Doesn't this sound like what we already saw in the garden of Eden and the life of Solomon?

René Descartes (1596–1650) has been regarded as "the Father of Philosophy," and he was one of the foundational contributors to the Enlightenment area and the philosophy of rationalism. Rationalism by definition, according to the *Merriam-Webster* dictionary, is "a reliance on reason as the basis for establishment of religious truth, a theory that reason is in itself a source of knowledge superior to and independent of sense perceptions, a view that reason and experience rather than the nonrational are the fundamental criteria in the solution of problems."

As the Enlightenment progressed, the focus on reason as the guiding force in our human experience was further explored, and many philosophers of the time began to realize that reason alone would ultimately lead to not only trouble but also evil decision-making (sin). In one of his latter works, *Religion within the Limits of Reason Alone* (Kant 1793), Immanuel Kant said, "Hence we can call this a natural propensity to evil, and as we must, after all, ever hold man himself responsible for it, we can further call it radical innate evil." In summary, reason without God is very dangerous indeed. When we rely on our own intelligence, we start to fall in the same trap as Solomon. We are absolutely ripe for the devil's attacks. Also much like Adam and Eve, when we start to listen to each other's bad ideas and cosigning the sin, we as a human species have an innate condition toward bad, which is a form of evil, which in turn is outside of God's will, which equals sin. The Enlightenment thinkers by majority were not out to tarnish Christianity as much as to attack the overruling corruption that they saw religious leaders wielding along with what they perceived as man's laziness to grow as a species and use their intellect with centuries of knowledge and budding science at their disposal.

"Religious thought during the Enlightenment attempted to destroy traditional religion, Christianity, and build a new religion based upon an earthly foundation" (Jeremiah Grosse).

The Enlightenment came on the heels of the Reformation, which saw the split of the Protestants away from the Catholic Church. We had already begun to reject organized religion because we were judging the leaders involved and real or perceived corruption of the gospel as taught in the Bible by their actions and lack of adherence to it. The Enlightenment began a process that in many ways encouraged people that they need to fix themselves, that if they applied reason and science to their human problems, then they could become better versions of their own self, that they could be cured of whatever it was that plagued them. According to this philosophy of thinking, that was truly the goal in life—be the best you can be by identifying your problems and in your own strength using logic and science become better. It is not hard to see how this has affected the world we live in today. Man, have we overshot the mark so many times in so many ways! Modern psychology, meditation, and medications—they can be such an amazing blessing to be able to help those that suffer. However, if they are all you have, my experience is that the results never last. You have tried to fix yourself just as the Fathers of the Enlightenment hoped you would; but sadly without God, and I mean God as in the Father, Son, and Holy Spirit, you will inevitably yearn for more or feel like you are missing something that would give you joy. And the truth is my friend, you are.

CHAPTER 6

Finding Christ

I live a life today that is not controlled by my past. The mistakes and bad choices in my life before accepting Christ have all been brought to Him, and they no longer have any power over me. I have acknowledged to Jesus my sins, and I have also forgiven many people that hurt me and also myself for my part in all those relationships. Today I truly live a life of freedom and happiness because I allow God to do the work in and to me that needs to take place. Again, I no longer fill a God-sized hole other than with God to the best of my abilities. I have to remember that and live that at all costs to keep the freedom He has given me, and the best way to keep this gift is to give it away as I am attempting to do with these very words to you.

It is a daily exercise to stay spiritually fit and connected to God. I have to maintain my sobriety, both physically and emotionally, and I have to seek time with God through scripture, prayer, and meditation on Him. I start and end the day in prayer where I ask the Holy Spirit to make me aware of any selfish thinking or wrongs done throughout the day. I didn't create this process. Many successful recipients of a relationship with God before me found this to be a successful approach to a Spirit-filled life. Again, this is one of those junctures in my twelve-step program that seeks that you find a higher power, and my growth that led me to Jesus Christ formed an incredibly symbiotic relationship. If you think about God and how loving He is, then this isn't really complicated to understand. He works things out perfectly, and He gives us the ability to have our own personal relationship with Him as long as we seek it with our hearts and take the next action He places on us.

If we step back to the time period I wrote about in chapter 4, where I talked about lying in bed sleepless at night seeking God, I can tell you two things. The first is that at that time I was completely miserable! I was exhausted both mentally and physically from the last several years of stress, and I felt that there was not a path forward for me that included anything that I wanted to be happy. Not only was I desperate for God, but I also needed Him more than ever because I didn't see a way forward in my own strength. Life was too much to bear without some kind of energy and hope that I currently didn't possess. I didn't want to go backward into active addiction, but I also had absolutely no idea how to move forward sober with no life. By no life, I literally mean I was stuck dreading the next morning because it meant I had to go through the whole day again wondering, *Seriously, what is the point? You have ruined your life! But you are still here walking around in it.* Yes, it was depressing, and no, I never thought of suicide simply because I am sure God made sure I didn't consider that. I wasn't likely someone who would fail to pull it off. God did however have a death in mind for me. That was all part of His plan for my life. He needed me to seek Him wholeheartedly. As the scripture says, "For whoever wishes to save his life will lose it; but whoever loses his life for My sake will find it. For what will it profit a man if he gains the whole world and forfeits his soul?" (Matthew 16:24–25 NASB).

I literally felt the presence of God. As I mentioned, I would lay in bed at night with rapid and continuous thoughts of despair. I would get to these points of heightened heart rate, discomfort, anxiousness, and utter despair; and I would say, "God, please reveal yourself to me." On several occasions, all those feelings would stop, and I would see two powerful eyes looking back at me. It would jolt me. I was undeniably in the presence of something way more powerful than me that was outside of myself. I would love to say that it was a comforting feeling, but what I truly felt was power so far beyond myself that it was difficult to even be in His presence. Those events began to change me. I was sure that not only had God existed, but also He was all powerful. He was also present with me where I was. It was exactly what I needed at that juncture to begin to grow a heart ready to receive Jesus.

It would be almost two years later from those days in Mount Pleasant, South Carolina, that I was born again, but it was just around the corner. I just couldn't see it yet. I praise Jesus so often that He met me where I was. God truly revealed Himself to me in a way that was irrefutable (yes, of course, I was a little afraid I was losing my mind), but the experience was and still remains to be a very crucial part of who I am today.

CHAPTER 7

Modern Day

For everything in the world—lust of the flesh,
the lust of the eyes, and the pride of life—comes
not from the Father but from the world.

—1 John 2:16 NIV

I look around today, and it is obvious to me why so many people are anxious and depressed. They are constantly viewing their self-worth and adjusting their ideals and principles based off the information they are inundated with. There is a lot of high-speed visual noise today. The advent of the Internet and smartphones led to an information revolution and social media accounts. We can now see what everyone with a profile or Twitter account is doing in real time, and the old saying "bad news travels fast" is literally a matter of seconds or minutes now. This is not completely a bad thing. It can be used for incredibly good such as when a person needs an organ or support after a disaster or when a whole community needs healing like after a school or church shooting like what happened after the shooting at Emanuel AME in Charleston, South Carolina. Thousands upon thousands poured in their support as the images and messages flew across our screens. God used that moment to unify many and soften hearts to the reality of evil in the world.

There is however another side of all this, and that is what the devil uses. The devil is called the "ruler of the world" (Belial in Hebrew and also 2 Corinthians 6:15) for a reason, and he is also called the great deceiver who prowls around like a lion seeking to destroy us (1 Peter 5:8 NASB). I was blessed to have an addiction that made me become self-aware that I was incredibly self-centered and selfish. Humans today face a major challenge. They see what they think is happiness in someone else's pictures, may it be a boyfriend/girlfriend, a family, an exotic location, a party, someone living a life of luxury, or even someone who looks to be a stoic monk. It doesn't matter what it is, but the majority of the time, you are only getting part of the picture. What you typically see is a billboard! "This is how amazing I am and look how awesome and happy I am." But what you don't see is what is in that person's soul. If it is not God, then I can promise you they are not fulfilled in some area of themselves whether they are currently aware of it or not. I have known many cases were the person you see online and the actual individual's life are incredibly different. Social media profiles can be much like going to Disney World. Everything looks absolutely amazing, tangible, and even palpable, but if you inspect closer, the majority of it is a façade to an empty or blank wall behind it. What you see are the colorful props and sets. There is also a level of playing victim or humble that can be quite silly if you step back. I remember years ago (when I had a social media account) a person posted how they were late for work, stuck in traffic, and just spilled their coffee. I wanted to say, "Then why in the world are you on here right now?" It's a silly example but people post their meagerness sometimes to get reactions and feel better about themselves.

God intended for humans to have community with one another (Ephesians 4:12–16). He also allowed us to be smart enough to create amazing things as we discussed in earlier chapters, but as we also discussed earlier, we have yet again stepped into the devil's trap. Our selfie world is struggling with its identity again. We go to such extremes to show how wonderful we are that has led to incredible harm. Suicides, depression, and anxiety are on the rise. Addiction is rampant and not just in the traditional sense. People cannot stop looking at social media and posting and commenting. There is no last word or end of the story as we are continuously inundated with more and more information. Yes, some of it is real and important, but the "devil is in the details." We clamor to have the inside scoop, the new information, the most profound post about it, and on and on we go. This isn't new, for humans have loved gossip forever; however the speed and ease at which we receive this information have trapped us before we even know we are hooked. Just look at the next factual event that occurs and attempt to watch from the sidelines at how emotion-filled and consumed everyone becomes and then recognize that in some period of time, may it be days, weeks, or months the majority of enraged commenters that didn't do any actual actions to better the situation have moved on to something else that appears by their post is of the utmost importance to them.

I don't want to get too into the weeds on this as that can be a sticky subject because there definitely are very just causes out there that people do need to focus on such as equality, respect, and love for all. This does not however mean that we should attempt to justify sin just because the tidal wave of social movements demand that we accept things that are outside of God's will. These in my opinion are the obvious cases. Now let's look at where the devil is much more subtle in his attacks that get people angry and confused.

How much time have you spent in the last day looking at a social media account? How long do you scroll through posts and people's pictures in an hour, a day, a week, or a year? The moments of viewing posts and pics add up to real amounts of time. Let us just say, for a modest example, you look at it just twenty minutes a day. Well, that's almost 122 hours or 5 days a year! Spending five days a year doing anything would obviously have some kind of an effect on you, but if you have such accounts, you're likely looking at them much more daily. What are you doing on your spiritual condition daily? Yes, goat yoga may bring you zen and riding your motorcycle on a mountain road gives you a rush and a feeling of escape, but I am talking about spending time with God. How many minutes a day are you doing that? How are you doing it? Are you checking in with God as often as you're checking that social media account for comments, likes, and new posts?

As I started getting sober, the members of my twelve-step fellowship asked me an interesting question. "I know you don't always like going to meetings, working the steps, etc., but how long did you use to spend each day drinking?" "I would venture to guess we are asking you to do a lot less than you spent doing that to be free of it." We need to unplug from this chaos and get our bearings if we plan on growing into happier and healthier people. In later chapters, I will discuss in my detail how I was able to begin and live this process, but it is crucial that we identify the problem first. I will admit I used to live a life that went from chaos to chaos. Sadly I had become rather good at it, and unfortunately, it made me feel alive on some level. The truth however is this. I found that all these pursuits and desires to be a part of the world's social fabric often left me angry, dismayed, and alienated. I was fairly anxious and never felt like I was truly "like" anyone else or that they could like me in return. I was chasing my tail, to put it simply. There was no destination. The faster I spun, the more I thought I was getting somewhere. There is a great verse for this, and Solomon calls these earthly pursuits, "chasing the wind" (Ecclesiastes 2:11 NLT). We live in a world today that is filled with chasing the wind. I honestly believe that we have come to such a point of trying to perfect ourselves that we began to listen to many of the devil's lies. It feels so much easier to jump on the bandwagon of what society tells you is correct. There is a sense of acceptance and relief that you finally belong. The problem is this part of our being was not intended to find peace here on earth. It was meant for us to have fellowship and to worship and gain peace from God. There is a reason we all yearn so much to fill the lonely holes inside of ourselves, and the most extreme cases of these yearnings ultimately find themselves in isolation because they simply cannot seem to fit in anywhere else. This isolation may be physical, but it is often isolation in plain sight. People get a reward from attention on social media—I mean an actual immediate reward that keeps them hooked every time someone receives a like online. Studies have shown that it releases dopamine in the brain. Dopamine is the brain's natural way to reward you for good behavior, such as eating, drinking water when thirsty, sleeping, and appropriate sexual activity. If you walk back through that short list, you can see how when these activities are overstimulated, addictions are formed.

Sean Parker, a cofounder of Facebook, in 2018 said,

> How do we consume as much of your time and conscious attention as possible? It was this mindset that led to the creation of features such as the "like" button that would give users "a little dopamine hit" to encourage them to upload more content.

> It's a social-validation feedback loop... exactly the kind of thing that a hacker like myself would come up with, because you're exploiting a vulnerability in human psychology. (*The Guardian*, Sun, March 4, 2018)

It is no surprise that social media has had a profound impact on our lives, but sadly most people would prefer to send a text these days than have a conversation all because we got so used to doing it online.

I often find myself frustrated with what I hear people say about their beliefs. The frustration comes that often these beliefs are based off what they encounter online and on the news, and they are typically very polarized. We live in a time and era that people are so overwhelmed with the amount of information that we get lost from how we really feel or even think. Topics of contention are hammered by so many comments and criticisms that the majority of people make up their minds on major issues based off the social tide and the information it has provided them. I also believe, from my own experience, that people can become glamorized by feeling like they are a part of some great movement and begin to compromise what they know to be wrong or inappropriate behavior. People can also get laser-focused on the actions of others in an unconscious attempt to take attention off themselves. I also feel like I see people cosign inappropriate behaviors or beliefs in an attempt to keep people off their back. It's kind of like, "Oh, if I show how supportive I am of X, they won't see my personal problem with Y." As an example, someone may take to social media talking about the importance of equality, while at the same time, they are not actually practicing it in their own marriage. I think we are all guilty of these redirections, myself included. Elizabeth is really good at making me aware of the fact that I may be incredibly patient with a complete stranger, yet I will expect something of her that is not patient in the least. I think my defensive response to this would be that she knows better from our previous discussions as a couple or that I think she should be "healthier" than anyone else. The intention of this may be genuine, but it is easy to see that it is not fair.

Our world today is a high-speed façade of what life is supposed to be to make you happy—glamorous, exciting, and sexy. Elizabeth and I like to watch a survival show occasionally where they are in Alaska. It looks so simplistic and almost romantic to be so far removed. We get tickled sometime imagining what the rest of the year looks like when the camera isn't there. I think I would ultimately become mute or go insane. As a family, we definitely wouldn't like it 365 days a year. I find myself wondering, What is the point? I can however do the same thing when I look at people who have reached the apex of success and spend their days, well, spending and traveling. Having had a taste of that in my own life, I can 100 percent guarantee you it is not all sunshine and glamour. You can actually be so consumed by the whole experience of luxury where it begins to get boring and you can't seem to put your finger on it but it's just not good enough. As I said previously, this doesn't fly in the face of wonderful experiences. It just reminds us that God warns us against idolatry (Exodus 20:4). Don't throw the book out thinking I am telling you to never go on vacation again. We have created our own image of God here on earth with the perceived amazingness of who we are. We think we have grown so socially acceptable that we are instilling true love to one another while arguing all the way. God is the only true source of peace and purpose; after all He created us. I think the modern age inundating us with information has caused a large fracture in the fissure of humankind and the image of God. Now for the good news! There is hope.

CHAPTER 8

Here and Now

I was baptized on May 5, 2017. It's not easy to remember because it was Cinco De Mayo, but it's easy to remember because it was the day before Elizabeth and I got married. All of my family and closest friends were there, and Pastor Fant who had done our premarital counseling was able to see the Holy Spirit work in a man who he had invested his love for Christ. It was an amazing day and an exhilarating experience. Everything changed after that, and the symbolic dunk in the sea was my public confirmation that I had accepted Jesus Christ as my Savior and Lord, but when I say everything changed, I mean life changed drastically. Yes, I was free of major emotional burdens and wounds that had plagued me for many years of my life, but what was about to take place almost seems counterintuitive.

We got pregnant on the honeymoon! It was a big surprise because we thought with Elizabeth's family history, it may be a difficulty for us. I then felt my calling to ministry and committed to such, and then our restaurants took a total nose-dive. It all seemed confusing, and it was happening at a dizzying rate. Within a year and a half, we would be contemplating a major move, struggling financially after trying to save the business, and looking for a new career. But before we get into that, let's back up a little bit and discuss God's presence in all this.

One powerful moment worth sharing is this. In the summer after our honeymoon, we were at the beach with my parents. As I liked to do, I would go down to the beach and spend time in prayer in the morning, giving gratitude to God for all He was doing in my life. One day, I went to pray and it was very different than the rest. I was finishing praying, and a thought came to me that was completely outside of myself and random. I didn't hear anything audibly, but the thought was, "You will have a child, and it will be a son." Honestly, at the time, I smiled and thought, *Wouldn't that be amazing? I really want a son.* I came back to the house to find that Elizabeth wasn't feeling well, and she wasn't sure what was wrong. A couple of days later, I walked into our bedroom at my parents' beach house, and she completely surprised me with two positive pregnancy tests in her hand. I had to sit down. *Wow, what a moment!* I remember it as if it was today. I laughed and cried, and after a minute or so, I looked at her and said, "It's going to be a boy." That obviously got her attention, and I explained to her how I was sure. Over the next weeks, people cautioned us not to get our hopes up (because I told everyone it was going to be a boy), and I can tell you that I really didn't question what God had shared with me one time! Yes, we had a boy on the way. Yes, I know because God told me that.

After some months, I had found myself becoming obsessive about understanding the Bible more. I felt a real desire to learn as much as I could to grow in my relationship with the Lord and also to better help others, which God had already begun using me for that purpose.

The dawn of a new existence was on the horizon, and before I truly knew what was happening, I was following a path that if you had told me would be a pursuit in my life back in 2012, I would have laughed at you and then told you to f—— off most likely. I wasn't an angry guy back then (at least not unless you made me mad), but I did cuss a lot joking around. I was going to seminary.

Pastor Fant and his wife came to visit us in Atlanta. We had been married about six months, and Elizabeth was pregnant enough to show. Charles and I sat outside by a fire on the back deck and talked. He was very much my first father in my relationship with Jesus, and we were having a healthy check-in. Something had been on my heart, and I let it rip about midevening. I said, "Charles, how do I go to seminary?" With that, he began to cry, and I didn't think this to be a good thing at first blush. I must have crossed the line. He caught himself and looked at me and told me how magnificent God had been. He had been praying that one day I would show some interest in seminary, asking, "How do I go?" was a completely different animal altogether, and he had just been blessed with an answered prayer. So he suggested Southwestern Baptist Theological Seminary, and after some prayer and research, I began the application process. This was a fun challenge, and why I share it here is that God was ever present in it.

First off, Elizabeth and I went to tell my parents what we were up to. Amazingly, my mom said, "You're going to be a pastor," before we could tell her and it blew everyone's mind. Dad was also very moved by it all and thought it was absolutely wonderful. That was a huge encouragement to me. Next after completing the whole application, I had one item left—the church recommendation. At this point, I had joined First Baptist Atlanta, but at the time, Dr. Charles Stanley was our pastor, and understandably it wasn't like you could just call him up and meet. So I pondered and prayed what to do. The people at FBA hardly knew me at this point, and they only knew I was the guy Elizabeth married as she used to work there.

Here is how God showed up. I had all but given up on someone from FBA writing my letter of recommendation and was going to ask Pastor Fant to do so. Then I received a text from Anthony George who at the time was the associate pastor of FBA (now senior pastor). Anthony and I had spoken a month before and had planned to get lunch, but it had fallen off both of our radars with the business of life. He and I sat down the next day, and I completely surprised him with my call to ministry and desire to go to SWBTS. Here is God— Anthony had been contacted by the president of SWBTS earlier that week requesting that he come visit. Long story short, Elizabeth and I were eating lunch in the house of the president of SWBTS two weeks later. I was so nervous that I looked him up. This was an old business practice I had before meeting with someone, try to find some common thread for a conversation. Here is God again. The man was an avid hunter who was seldom seen without his black Lab around campus, and we were great friends already. I am on my sixth black Lab since birth, who is my hunting dog!

Elizabeth sat in the car the majority of the tour. A better description was she laid back with the front seat reclined in the car. She was seven and a half months pregnant at the time, and we literally had to check and see if she could still fly on Delta to come out to Texas based on her later stage of pregnancy. I remember like it was yesterday. When we first got there, I turned back around and walked back to the car and said, "What if these guys don't like me?" She replied, "You are here to serve God, not them." Later in the tour, I came back out after feeling completely energized. I had become nervous again. What in the world was I doing in a seminary? We were in the very impressive modern chapel, and at the height of my doubts, I turned around to a stained-glass window. Dr. Stanley was saying, "Trust God and leave all the consequences to Him." That rang my spiritual bell. I came over to the car and said, "Sweetie, I feel so called to be here." This time Elizabeth said, "Then let's move here." My jaw dropped and all I said was, "What?" She was clearly very convicted by the Holy Spirit, and it was such a beautiful (and terrifying) thing to witness. God had brought me so much more in my wife than a partner, best friend, and mother of my children. She was also here to help shape this man into God's image for Him and His purposes.

We had an awesome experience the rest of our visit and went home trying to figure out how we could rent a place in Fort Worth and travel back and forth. God had a very different plan in mind. As we were to soon find out, the restaurants that had been showing signs of less profits were about to take a nose-dive. As the months passed, we found me in seminary as an online student, a young baby boy had arrived, and I was trying to figure out how we could save the restaurants. Well, that part didn't happen. We lost over a million dollars and had to borrow money from Dad to even get out of the businesses a year later. Around that time, Dad had been looking for a new farm. I grew up going to a beautiful farm our family owned, and it was very much a part of my upbringing to spend lots of time there playing, hunting, fishing, and working in the summers in high school. I had truly missed our place, which had been sold a couple of years earlier, but it has always been amazing to me to reflect on the fact that the old farm had to go for God to move both me and my family into a different season of our lives. Dad had looked at about a hundred properties, no joke, and I think the actual number was 113. He had found a place, and we had gone to look at it together. I agreed. "Dad this is it!" I said, making sure the brokers didn't hear me fifteen feet away. I began to help him do the due diligence for the property, and at the same time, we were really getting very stressed about our future.

One evening, I was researching the property and area for Dad, and Elizabeth walked through the kitchen and said, "Honey, can I say something without you getting defensive?" Hesitantly I agreed. She said, "I know you don't want to go back into land brokerage, but everyone has told me you're very good at it. I have walked through the kitchen several times in the last two hours, and every time I come through, I look over at you researching that property and you have a smile on your face. Why not sell that kind of land?"

I looked up at here and said, "Honey, you're right. If you had asked me just yesterday, I would have kicked against the goads yet again, but I, too, have been asking myself the same thing for the last twenty minutes, and prayerfully I cannot come up with one reason why I shouldn't do this kind of brokerage."

Around that same period of time, I had finished working out one morning and found myself on my knees, out of breath, lamenting to God, "God, what do we need to do? We are going broke, and there is no solution in sight." God very clearly put on my heart, "Sell your house." The pieces were all coming together. In January 2019, we didn't know what to do, and in May 2019, we moved to Columbus, Georgia.

CHAPTER 9

The Awakening

I have had a discomfort with modern society that has bothered me for some time now. It ultimately was part of the catalyst for this book. I used to live so disconnected from God that I was just part of the machine, but now I so clearly see standing on the sidelines and watching in utter angst what a mess it all can be. My angst is not out of fear or anxiety. It is because I know that there is a better way to live that has freedom and purpose. The more I lean into living that life, the happier I truly am. That is because it is the life that God intended for me. Our world is vigilantly focused on the happenings around us, but we are completely blind to the real problems at hand. We play whack-a-mole with what we see right in front of us, but if we were to slow down, we would realize that we just need to unplug the machine to stop the intruder. So what is the machine and how do we disconnect from playing its game?

The first step to this is realizing that we have a problem and that the only way to change that problem is to stop feeding it. There is an old parable that is most popularly attributed to the Native Americans called the tale of two wolves, and it goes like this.

An old Cherokee told his grandson, "My son, there is a battle between two wolves inside us all. One is evil. It is anger, jealousy, greed, resentment, inferiority, lies, and ego. The other is good. It is joy, peace, love, hope, humility, kindness, empathy, and truth."

The boy thought about it and asked, "Grandfather, which wolf wins?"

The old man quietly replies, "The one you feed."

In study one day, I came across the apostle Paul's writings in the book of Romans, specifically Romans 8. Paul was the epitome of a sinner. He was a well-educated Jew (named Saul) whose goal in life was to destroy Christianity until the day Jesus struck him blind on the road to Damascus (Acts 9). From that day forward, Saul became Paul and wrote a large majority of the New Testament with the guidance of the Holy Spirit. Paul has a very similar opinion of these "two wolves" we just mentioned, and he speaks of our own bondage to self and sin often in his teachings (Romans 8:1–8), always pointing to the necessity to become followers of Christ's teachings and a vessel for Him to use (Romans 8:9–14). He speaks of the need for us to die to our old ways (Romans 8:13). Paul is acknowledging that we have a sinful nature in our flesh, and if we act out of this sinful nature, it creates evil and controls us. If however we die to that sinful nature, by seeking Jesus, we can be set free from its grip and begin to live a life that serves God's purposes. Paul doesn't lead us to believe that this life will be easy. To the contrary, he talks of the difficulties in multiple letters to the churches in Corinth, Galatia, and Ephesus, that is, the Bible books of Corinthians, Galatians, and Ephesians.

As a society, we have become so glued to what everyone is saying. The latest foul ball tweet, comment, post, or action in a Snapchat throws us in an absolute tizzy. We get mad, we get anxious, we feel like we have to respond, we have to keep watching, or we are a part of this. But what are we doing? In my opinion, we are letting the devil play us like a fiddle. Unless God tells you that you are supposed to take something on, unless you yourself are healthy enough spiritually to engage in all this action, then you are simply going to get consumed by it. I am well aware that there are many people reading this very sentence that probably think I am being too sensitive, pacifist, or even avoidant not to want to gravitate to join into a major social-media-driven stance on issues. Dare I even say they would think that I must be a bigot because of my silence. None of this could be further from the truth. If God has not put it on my heart to engage in a cause, I no longer pursue it. It can be really difficult to stay out of giving personal opinions, hyperfocusing on all the "news," but I have found it is a distraction that can consume me and quickly quench my spiritual flames.

What has happened in my life is I have been blessed to wake up to the fact that all the social chatter and noise are not healthy for me. If I engage in all the opinions and the ever-running jump from one perceived injustice to the next that the news or social media throws at us, I simply become part of tide of the masses, which lately sure doesn't seem to be God's direction. We have to find a way to stay grounded in what God wants for us to focus on, what God finds to be important issues, and that is not to say it is never what we think is important. But I can promise you this—if there are arguing, shaming, blaming, and demands for social hanging involved, then it is not likely that we are on course with Jesus's teachings, as He said, "He who is without sin among you, let him be the first to throw a stone at her" (John 8:7 NASB). Obviously, there are times that we should stand for some things, but I honestly believe a large majority acting out online have simply found it as yet another way to stay relevant and get attention on themselves, or sometimes the case is to get attention off themselves!

CHAPTER 10

Living in the Solution

I once heard a fun illustrative analogy about a ship being off course that I have adjusted over time to my own, and it goes like this. "If you are a couple of degrees off sailing a boat from Charleston, South Carolina, to a port in England, you are probably going to be a good bit off. (Maybe even end up in the wrong country.) You're not likely to reach your intended destination. Now if you are a couple of degrees off walking across the room, you are likely still going to make the doorway." Today I try to live in the latter, and when I realize I am off course, I do what needs to be done promptly to get back on course.

In order to stay spiritually healthy, I have to practice a daily connection with God that contains several important elements for me. Every person needs to prayerfully figure out what works for them. I would love to say that every day I do this perfectly and have a flawless regimen, but somedays are much better than others. I do however always start the day connecting with God as quickly as possible. I invite Him into my awareness and try to remove as much of myself as possible to let His will flow through me that day for His purposes. Yes, of course I am not a monk, and I live a life full of modern distractions and activities, but I truly believe that having a heart for God's will and not my own is a 100 percent successful day as opposed to the other.

I call myself a member of a twelve-step fellowship that by its very traditions state that it should stay anonymous. I am however allowed to share with you that I myself identify as an alcoholic and will forever owe my life to the program God put me in so that I could stay sober and grow spiritually enough to truly find Him. People have asked me, "If you have such a thriving relationship with Jesus Christ, why do you need to do those meetings?" And I tell them, "Because I found Him by staying sober through those meetings and working the twelve steps, and Jesus has never told me to stop going!" To answer the question more frankly, of course Jesus has the power to keep me sober; however, He has chosen that my path include the rooms that I frequent several times a week. I have a fellowship where I can feel at home anywhere in the world, not matter the culture or language. How amazing is that! We often open or close meetings with the serenity prayer written originally by Reinhold Niebuhr:

> God grant me the serenity
> to accept the things I cannot change;
> the courage to change the things I can;
> and the wisdom to know the difference.
>
> Living one day at a time;
> enjoying one moment at a time;
> accepting hardships as the pathway to peace;
> taking, as He did, this sinful world
> as it is, not as I would have it;
> trusting that He will make all things right
> if I surrender to His will;
> that I may be reasonably happy in this life,
> And supremely happy with Him
> forever in the next.
> Amen.

As I am writing this book, I am literally a month away from having to potentially declare bankruptcy after an almost two-year-long battle to get clear of four failed restaurants. We lost over a million dollars trying to right the ship and save them the first year of our marriage, and it was simply a lost cause that cost us all our money.

We had to borrow from my parents, and ultimately I am now trying to get us out of several million dollars in debt with $12,000 dollars left in the bank. I am blessed to be in a great new career selling recreational land, hunting plantations, timber tracts, and some commercial properties. But this is 2020, and COVID-19 has wreaked havoc on our world! I haven't had a deal close for six months, and that wasn't the plan. We have taken each next step trying to work through the debt with the bank, but currently there is no solution or end in sight and millions of dollars still to be cleared for us to move on. So we have nowhere to turn at this point but our faith. I once laughed with Elizabeth (and praise Jesus it was laughter, for there has been much stress and tears). I told her (stupidly), "We'll get through this. Trust me God has brought me through a lot." And here is the bad part. I added, "You just haven't been through anything tough like this." She looked at me and said, "Benjamin, in the last three years I have gotten engaged to a man with a scary past, married, pregnant, my husband was called to be a minister, our company failed, we lost a ton of money and a livelihood, had a baby, then got pregnant again, and then we sold our house and moved. I haven't been through anything?"

God, she was so right and I was so completely wrong. For all the young men out there, please let God help you find a woman like my wife. Every time I get insecure, she is quick to tell me in a very loving but matter-of-fact way that absolutely blows my mind. I often tell people that I am very blessed to have a gorgeous wife, and she also happens to be beautiful on the exterior. Elizabeth truly lived the easier and softer way than me. She knew Christ from a young age and never found it necessary to ever touch a drug or stay in an unhealthy relationship. Talk about opposites in that regard!

It dawned on me in the middle of a stressful couple of days worrying about our finances that I had forgotten something very simple that I had learned along the way. It was times like these in sobriety that I remember the real gift I have been given in Christ to be free of the bondage of self and substances. See for me, it is so easy to stay sober physically these days when things are tough. Life is happening in a way that is stressful and difficult to bear. In these times, it is obvious to me that to drink, drug, cheat, lie, etc. would absolutely make matters worse. It is however in these moments that my faith is tested, much like the struggles that Job went through in the Bible or like when Peter asked Jesus if he can walk on water and then lacked faith and started sinking once he had already walked several steps. The waves and the wind scared him, and he started sinking due to his disbelief and screamed, "Lord save me" (Matthew 15:29–31). I get like that with my faith sometimes. See there is a bizarre juxtaposition in me. When things are really tough, it is clear to me that to drink or use drugs would just make things worse. In comparison when things are going great is when I worry about my sobriety, because I just might get comfortable and confident enough that maybe I can let my program fall off a bit. In that same time period, I have absolutely no challenges of my faith, and it is rock-solid and vibrant. Turn the tables and the opposite is true. I start getting fearful when I am stressed. I have to remind myself that God never changes, and He is always there and always the same by His very nature. He also knows exactly how whatever I am going through is going to end and as we see David exult in Psalm 143:5–6, "I remember the days of old; I meditate on all thy doings… My soul longs for thee, as a parched land."

If you have let God into your life, you have proof that He moves on your behalf. He has brought you through such amazing trials, loss, and despair before, so why would He be different now? Gain strength in where He has helped you in the past. However, if you were like me, you probably didn't realize it many times, but you just pawned it off as luck or even worse your great achievement! God is the source of everything. We must invite Him into all the situations in life through prayer and honesty. You might as well. He already knows the truth! Pray to Him as if you were talking to your Creator right in front of you, because you are, and don't question that for a second. Just do it. In the scariest hours of my life, I hoped God heard me and that He cared. Now I know that God hears me and that He loves me and cares very much. What a relief! I used to think I had to take on the world myself, but now I know that I will fail or falter if I do not rely on God's strength to go through life's hard times.

CHAPTER 11

What Do We Do?

No change = no change

The more I grow spiritually, the more I realize that I still have to give up. I was almost comfortable with many years of therapy that made me realize the healthy and unhealthy elements of my family, the same things about myself, the parts of my own addictive nature that I had to learn to accept, and the selfish and self-centered nature of my existence that I had to be patient, loving, kind, and forgiving to others and that I had to forgive myself even to move forward and grow in life. But in order to do all this, I had to genuinely forgive. I had to remove all resentments, and I had to be willing to let all this go in a way that I was never capable of before. The devil had a very real trap set for me, and I need something more powerful to be free of all this. What I needed was Jesus Christ. I needed to be born again. "God sent his Son into the world not to judge the world, but to save the world through him [Jesus]" (John 3:17).

Before I accepted Christ, I had a dilemma. I would muster all my strength and make great efforts to forgive others and myself. Sometimes I even felt as if I had succeeded, but this was a deception. In time, something would happen, the thought would start to return, and ultimately, I would end up stuck in a cycle of thinking about what it was again, reanalyzing it as if this time the thoughts and feelings would allow me peace and closure. This was never the case, and all that thinking and feeling would just take the hurt, anger, and grief further down the road to a new distorted destination. I often explain it to guys I work with like this—imagine that painful thought is like a train, and you are standing at the station. You have ridden this train many times, and it never takes you anywhere good. Yet you continue to get on it, and around and around bad memory town you go until ultimately you are likely to act out in some unhealthy, "sinful" way not to feel or think that way for a bit. You want some feeling of escape or control. "By God, by now you deserve it," you proclaim. Well, we have to stop riding the train, bottom line. My experience has been through working my program of recovery and then taking these things to Jesus Christ, who suffered for me on the cross; acknowledging the sin (which is my part in the matter); asking Jesus to forgive me of this sin; and then asking Him to take it from me I am set free!

However, let's now go back to the station. That train (your thoughts or feelings of a past event) shows up again! Oh no! Taking it to Jesus didn't work. Well, that is not the truth. That is the devil and a little bit of psychology too. Firstly, the devil wants you to stay trapped, and secondly, you have conditioned your brain to fire a certain way when this event is brought to mind. The bottom line is this—if you have accepted Jesus Christ into your life and have taken this sin to Him who bled for you on the cross, acknowledged your part, and asked Him to forgive you and remove it from you, *it no longer has power over you* (1 John 5:9). But let's say you jump on the train anyway and decide to ride it several stops through bad memory town. So what? You haven't fallen backward. You just need to practice a little mindfulness and get off the train as soon as possible. The devil will want to pester you, and your brain is going to take time to heal. I want to be very clear—you will likely need to begin this work with someone qualified to help you, like a pastor or therapist, someone who can help you stay grounded in the present and work through any trauma that has not yet been processed. It has taken me many years of professional and spiritual help to get to a place where I can work on these things, and even today if something from my past comes up, I mention it to a trusted fellow man in my twelve-step recovery before talking to Jesus because there is something in that human connection that helps it come to the surface in a way that I can then hand it to God.

We have to be at a place of willingness for change. If you are like me, this will be a process that can take years. For me, it took the better part of a decade to develop to a point where I truly wanted spiritual growth. By growth, I mean taking the necessary actions to receive such growth. A plant without soil, water, and sun cannot grow. The right types of each determine the kind of growth that it has; the plant cannot be healthy without the proper environment. Sure it can grow without soil without lots of sun and with little water, but unless it has been artificially altered in some way, this plant is not going to thrive in those conditions. We are a little more complicated than plants, and that example is far from perfect, but the point is we need to place ourselves in the right environment to grow. A plant doesn't have to wake up each morning and decide it wants to be a better or happier plant to survive. But I sure did! I am blessed that my circumstances were so extraordinary that it was impossible to sell myself one more lie or excuse. This plant needed light (God/prayer), water (a purpose greater than myself), and great soil (a foundation of healthy fellowship). From that healthy plant, God began to bear fruit, and that is visible in the life that I have today—what really matters, what makes me excited to get at the day, and what God has given me that I couldn't give to myself! Depending on where you are in your journey, this may be more or less obvious to you. You may also feel deep down that you want this kind of joy and purpose, but it's just not possible. It's exhausting to think about all the change, it's scary to imagine failing, and you likely have failed previously at such attempts to change. It is never too far and never too late to grow into a healthier person. Just pray to be willing, and then take the next step. Don't worry about the destination. Just pray and take the next right step, but do it today, not tomorrow. If it helps, get on paper what you feel, where you want to be, and your willingness to pursue it. Even if it is just bullet points for now, have something to strive for that is a healthier version of yourself. You likely don't know him/her yet, so don't be afraid! It has been my experience that the thoughts of what are to come are typically far scarier than the reality. The devil is really good at using your own mind against you to create the perfect scenario of why you can't do something healthy. If you are stuck in addiction, you *have* to get out of that first for any of this to work. It's simply impossible to have true spiritual growth when your mind and body are under the influence of substances that alter your feelings and demand your consumption in order to feel "normal" again. What a lie that is, and many of us live it daily, if not hourly.

It gets easier, I promise. Just be willing, pray, and take the next step. If you relapse back into old behavior, *do not* be deceived that you failed. You just need to commit yourself a little more, a little longer. We are all at different places with this. I still strive to grow as much as I can daily. I view myself as a thousand miles from where I was, yet a million miles from the destination. However, I have learned how to enjoy the journey and live life in a state of gratitude and active anticipation for the next level of spiritual growth. This is incredibly rewarding! Never perfect, but that's not the goal either. It is all about the journey.

CHAPTER 12

The Eternal Life

For whoever wishes to save his life shall lose it; but
whoever loses his life for My sake and the gospel
shall save it. For what does it profit a man to gain
the whole world, and forfeit his soul Jesus Christ.

—Mark 8:35–56 (NASB)

As I hope I clearly stated in this book, finding Jesus for me was very much a process. This process was not what I was even thinking would happen, but through fervent praying for God to show me more of Himself, I began to grow spiritually. At first, this growth began as an eagerness to be a better man, and ultimately, God led me to the one truth that is the Gospel of Jesus Christ. Gospel literally means good news, so what is the good news of Jesus. In a nutshell, He conquered all sin that kept us separated from God. As I explained earlier, God cannot be in the presence of anything imperfect. By His very attributes, anything outside of His will be removed from existence. However, we were His creation and fell from perfection in the garden of Eden with mankind's first sin. Jesus restored our ability to have a direct relationship with God without being destroyed. His blood was traded for our imperfection/sin (Hebrews 10:19–23 NASB). Jesus restored our relationship with God through His suffering and death on earth as the final sacrifice. John the Baptist was given this knowledge as he said when first seeing Jesus, "Behold, the Lamb of God who takes away the sin of the world" (John 1:29 NASB).

I tell people all the time that I honestly never intended to find Jesus Christ and be baptized to symbolize that I had a desire to be born again as a follower of Jesus. This was the result of seeking God and being willing to let Him show me the truth, the good news, so to say. I can tell you that this transformation in my soul has opened the door to incredible freedom. Before I accepted Christ, I worked very hard in my own strength to be a better man and grow through past hurts, fear, and anger. The fortunate blessing is that I have come to realize that I now have the one power to release me from all this bondage, and that is a thriving relationship with Jesus Christ. It amazes me how many years I spent avoiding the one surrender that would set me free—oh yeah, let's not forget—and also give me eternal life in heaven (minor detail).

At this point, I hope you are excited and energized by the fact that you too know what I experience by having fellowship with Jesus, knowing God, and benefiting from the peace and purpose that brings. But what if you're not there? What if this all sounds like something you simply cannot do for x, y, and z? What if you have past experiences with religion that make you recoil or armor up when you hear the name Jesus Christ? What if you have a lot of ambitions for money, popularity, sex, and power left to accomplish and this all sounds like it is going to get in the way of that or try to make you feel bad about your actions? What if you have found that you like your current spiritual enlightenment and think that we should have a more universal approach, "all roads lead to heaven"? Well, other than the first experience mentioned, I was right there with you. Like I said previously—and this is all I am going to suggest to unbelievers that have read this far—be willing in your heart to consider who God truly is and who He is not. Start by praying for God to reveal to you more of Himself. Be willing to consider what you start to feel. Lean into the discomfort and the potential insecurity that this is silly (remember the devil doesn't want you to enjoy this process).

The following is a note to nonbelievers: If you are now ready to take the next step and accept Jesus Christ, see appendix A.

It is also important to remember this—we will all have some level of brokenness that we have to go through in order to know God. This is suffering, and for whatever reason, it simply is a part of life as we know it on earth. For me, the brokenness was over a decade of my life and truly grew more and more intense as the consequences of how I was living manifested bad and scary situations that were life-changing. The blessing in all this is that it doesn't take a long trip down memory lane to remember what it was like to live outside of God's will. I have said to Elizabeth before, "There is a great benefit to my past way of living. I have been down those dark alleys you were taught to avoid. I have had the experiences that I thought would give me satisfactions, and I have no desire to try any of it again, not even a curiosity." I have gained a better understanding through the hardships that I and those around me endured that have left a truth in me that to live that way is empty, fruitless, and depressing.

Today I live with Jesus as the vine that energizes me. Jesus said, "I am the true vine, and My Father is the vinedresser. Every branch in Me that does not bear fruit, He takes away; and every branch that bears fruit, He prunes it so that it may bear more fruit… If you abide in Me, and my words abide in you, ask whatever you wish, and it will be done for you" (John 15:1–2, 7 NASB). This is a really cool concept if you stop and think about it. If you seek God and God's will, He will bless you. What I have found that is truly wild about this is that when I seek God's will, He works on the desires of my heart, meaning this—I am not asking God for a new helicopter. Instead I truly want a purposeful life. I ask for God's will and direction, and He continues to bless me amazingly, well beyond what my flesh thought it wanted. Yes, there are times that I have desires of old, but those are usually times that I am having some spiritual warfare taking place. Times of immense stress, unanswered prayers, some disappointment, or boredom—these are moments that I can feel disconnected from God, but the miracle of my current relationship with Jesus is I can literally destroy these feelings of discontent with a small amount of spiritual work (Bible study, prayer, fellowship, and service). God uses these times to grow me.

How do I do this? This is a daily practice. However, I have a community around me that helps me remember to stay in these practices (Bible study, prayer, fellowship, and service). Let us start with Bible study. This used to seem like an intense and boring exercise that elders in the church or pastors undertook that didn't seem relevant to me. When I say Bible study, I mean several things. First getting something manageable, like a good daily devotional. There are many of them out there by many great Christian writers and pastors. The first one I had was *Jesus Calling.* It even comes in an app form. Another good beginning asset is the YouVersion app. This can be downloaded for free and provides a daily scripture and many Bible studies that are different lengths on different topics. I started with the electronic platforms to placate the electronically advanced, but I also highly suggest that you get a Bible. My first Bible was a Dr. Charles Stanley Life Principles Bible (NKJV). This was a wonderful start as it gave me commentary and explanations along with pertinent parts of the text I was reading. I personally now like the New American Standard Bible (NASB) as it is a very good modern translation that is most closely linked to the Greek and Hebrew original texts. There are many options out there like the NASB, NKJV, NIV, and NLT, which I have listed in order of how much they are paraphrased from the original text. I think finding a Bible that you can best understand while keeping as much to the original text is the goal here, and obviously there are several options that will also likely best fit where you are now.

I found the Bible to be overwhelming and confusing at first. The more I have studied it, the more it makes sense to me. A really fun element of studying the Bible is that as you begin to mature in your faith, the Holy Spirit speaks to you differently through the text and in different situations and seasons of life. This makes the scripture eternally useful and relevant.

Now for prayer. The way that I pray today is very different than how I prayed the majority of my life. It wasn't that I prayed as often for selfish things in my past, but it was more like a structured list of people that I would rattle off without any real meditation on what it was that I was saying. I was more so checking the box that I prayed before bed, and I would thank God or lament to Him about worries or things that I was scared of, but again it was me doing all the talking. I had no concept of how the Lord wants us to pray/worship Him. There are many scriptures on seeking the Lord, and here are a couple that help set the framework of how I have learned to pray.

> Seek the Lord while He may be found, call upon Him while He is near. (Isaiah 55:6 NASB)

> And I say to you, ask, and it shall be given to you, seek, and you shall find; knock, and it shall be opened to you. (Luke 11: 9 NASB)

> And in the same way the Spirit also helps our weakness; for we do not know how to pray as we should, but the Spirit Himself [Holy Spirit] intercedes for us with groanings too deep for words; and He who searches the hearts knows what the mind of the Spirit is, because He intercedes for the saints according to the will of God. And we know that God causes all things to work together for good to those who love God, to those who are called according to His Purposes. (Romans 8:26)

Here is how I have learned to pray, and I continue to learn daily. I approach God as my Creator, and I recognize that His grace and forgiveness are amazing. Then I ask the Holy Spirit to direct my heart and thoughts, and I begin to have a conversation with God. Much unlike the structured list of people and things that I used to rattle off each evening, I now have respectful fellowship with God.

I once had a pastor say something to me that was very profound. "Imagine that you are praying. How do you feel? Do you feel connected to Jesus or do you feel like you are speaking to an empty room?"

I said, "I feel like I am speaking to the Creator of the universe, but He definitely is far away from me yet present at the same time."

My pastor friend next asked me to imagine that Jesus Christ was sitting in the chair next to us. "Now how do you feel and what is different?" he asked.

I said, "I feel like I am having a conversation with God."

He said with a smile, "That's good, because you are."

What I learned in this moment and have carried forward is to approach Jesus as if I was physically present with Him and have a conversation with Him, a very respectful and honest one because He already knows the truth. Look back at the three scriptures I just provided above and take this away from them. God is here now, God knows your heart, the Holy Spirit will help you bring things to God, and God will answer your prayers if they are His will. Learn to pray for God's will, not your own. I know this sounds painful and sometimes it is, but I promise you if you do this, you will feel so much peace when you see what God is up to in your life. Unfortunately, the discomfort and struggle comes first because that is just part of being human.

On to having fellowship—for some reason when I hear the word *fellowship*, it still can sometimes make me feel uncomfortable, like it is some cheesy attempt at intimacy or community that ultimately has some kind of agenda or is going to ask too much of me or want something from me. True fellowship is a ridiculous blessing that I have come to cherish. I have best friends in sobriety and brothers in Christ that I confide in daily. At this point, there isn't anything that major going on typically, and this isn't about taking someone else's inventory or sharing overly private information about myself or my partner or gossip, even if there are times that I feel like that would be a good thing to share. I have had to learn over the years what appropriate fellowship is all about, and it is about having a common interest for spiritual growth that challenges us to grow. This growth comes from sharing with another "fellow" in this spiritual journey elements, thoughts, feelings, and desires appropriately in a safe environment that doesn't judge in order to further become a better man.

Again, this has taken me time to understand as I used to pride myself as a lone wolf alpha male, who needed to be loved but was always perplexed at how I couldn't obtain the love I so desperately desired. Well, the reason is I was unhealthy, spiritually sick as we call it in the rooms. In order to get out of this unhealthiness, I needed to surround myself with men who were healthier than me, or at least in that day and time, they were able to help me see what I knew to be true deep down inside but couldn't change as much as I wanted to. I had to learn how to look at myself in a new way, on the shoulders of those who had come before me that were able to share with me their experience and growth. I remember how absolutely uncomfortable this was at first and how dangerous to my pride and ego it would be for my deepest secrets, regrets, and thoughts to be found out, the things I was sure I would take to the grave; but the truth is in time I have learned that getting things off my chest, in the right setting, allows me to get them to God. God intended for us humans to have fellowship with one another, to help one another. As the apostle Paul said, "Each of us is to please his neighbor for his good, to his edification… And concerning you, my brethren, I myself also am convinced that you yourselves are full of goodness, filled with all knowledge and able also to admonish one another… For I will not presume to speak of anything except what Christ has accomplished through me, resulting in obedience of the Gentiles by word and deed" (paraphrased Romans 15:2, 3, 14, 18). Paul is talking about being Christ-centered and denying oneself on behalf of helping others. These are the people you are looking for. This is the fellowship you want to have. You need to find a group of individuals healthier than yourself who can help show you the way.

I want to clarify that for me, this started with a fellowship in twelve-step recovery that then has grown into a fellowship of Christian believers (and both are part of my balancing force today). I have a network of men to contact that I equate to a sports team bench. Each person on my bench has a specific area that they specialize in. Some men are fathers like me, some are pastors, others are businessmen, one is my actual father, but all are people that God has put in my life to help me stay on course. Like I said before, it is very difficult—actually impossible in my opinion—to be totally honest with yourself when you are trying to overcome some obstacle. We all need some guidance to learn that which is outside of ourselves. Here is the blessing in this that I have found. I am able to help the next guy grow now, and that helps me stay present with where God has brought me from, which in turn gives me incredible gratitude and peace.

Service can take place in many ways, and it evolves as we grow more in our relationship with Christ. To begin service, we often have to make someone aware that we want to do it in the first place. We have to be present for it. It is not likely that it is going to come seek you out. You may be thinking, I have a lot of hobbies and love to relax, or I am super active in athletic activities, such as fishing, hunting, and hiking. Well, less a couple of those, so am I! Service by its nature is doing something for others that requires us to make a sacrifice of our time and sometimes our money or livelihood. To be active in service successfully, you are making yourself fully available and focused to the cause in front of you. This is a process of giving back without the intent of receiving anything in return. Often the best service is done when no one even knows you did it, like helping an old lady take back her empty shopping cart. The moment you tell someone about it, you kind of take the humble servitude out of it and make it more about yourself and how nice you are. I am just beginning to work into this role of service. I even find myself feeling like my seminary studies in some regard are service as I am doing them to gain knowledge to better serve God and help others.

There are a lot of wonderful organizations out there doing great works of service in communities and on the mission field. I would suggest that you pray for where God wants you to be of service and see where He leads you. Case in point, before we moved to Columbus, Georgia, I had very little involvement with the veteran community other than one close friend. After moving here, I have been excited to see where I feel like God wants me to be involved in ministry, a very specific group of veterans that God has put on my heart. Not only has God put this on my heart, but He is also in the process of connecting me with the right people and has blessed me with access to a wonderful place for this ministry to take place. I continue to lean into where God wants to use me, and it has been a very humbling experience because to do it in His will, I have to really work to be present with my best attributes.

Now for the great news. Service done with a generous and genuine heart will bless you a thousandfold. It truly is wonderful the feeling of purpose that you have when you see that God has used you to help someone else. It gets you out of yourself (which is usually a much-needed vacation for many of us), and it gets you present with good. There is so much evil in this world, so to access the good is so vital for all of our well-being. This selflessness I have come to find keeps me grounded in the blessings that God has given me. It reminds me of His amazing grace and the power that He has to restore and shine and light in even the darkest of corners if we are willing to take it there. God intended for us to have fellowship with Him and a community of believers.

Conclusion

I felt that writing this book was something that served God and His purposes for my life. It is abundantly clear to me that God has a plan for me, and after many years of not living the life that best served his purposes, I have seen many different consequences, losses, and despair. I came from a place of feeling as if I lost everything, with no potential for a happy, purposeful future that would be anything like what I so dearly wanted to an existence today that far outreached my wildest dreams! I had no idea that in losing everything I held so dear, I would finally become happy. The reason for this happiness is that it is in God's will. He has blessed me with my current life with Christ, my wife, my sobriety, my children, my call to ministry, and my livelihood. I couldn't even see the life I have before. I mean literally I couldn't see myself past thirty-five years old, and I always just figured that meant I would die. Well, I did die, much in the way God warned Adam and Eve, "You will surely die if you eat that fruit." He meant spiritual death. My death however was to the self-centered, emotionally, and materialistically dependent self. I had to lose everything to gain it all as Jesus tells us is the case in Mark 8:35: "For whoever wishes to save his life will lose it, but whoever loses his life for my sake and the gospel's will save it." I had to lose my life as I knew it, and that process is far from over. It is almost daily that I find areas that I still need to surrender, things that I need to seek forgiveness for and let go, and ways that I need to change to better fit into the man God intends me to be.

We have covered several areas in this book and also looked at several great examples from the Bible and also the lens of modern philosophy/psychiatry and societal forces. God has created us! He has created us to glorify Himself (Isaiah 43:7). I used to have a real

BENJAMIN M. CARTER JR.

problem with this concept, but the more I grow and mature, the more I can proclaim God's amazing grace. Stop and think about this a moment. God made you, and without God's desire for you to exist, you simply wouldn't. Now consider this—God made you for a purpose. It is definitely His purpose, and you are likely either striving to find that or running like Jonah did.

As the story goes, God put Jonah where He wanted him to go. It may have taken him being thrown overboard and having to spend three days in the belly of a large fish (imagine how unpleasant that would be), but God got him there. After arriving in Nineveh, Jonah spoke to the people God sent him to preach to, and they all turned toward God. This was God's plan all along, but now even Jonah was upset as he didn't think they deserved it. He went and sulked on a hillside, and God had to bring him more discomfort for him to finally see that God's plan was the best plan and that by doing what God intended for him, great things have taken place. There was an absolute purpose and success to what Jonah had done, and it was God's will after all, so it was the best.

Where are you on your journey? I have tried to share my feelings and situations, and this book covers a decade of growth. This first half was all suffering and the latter all blessing and happiness, yet not free of stress and conflicts of its own. However, I can genuinely tell you that the life I am pursuing, the foundation of which has been substantially laid by God already. It's the most amazing and beautiful ride. I am trying my hardest to row and let God steer, and He takes us to amazing destinations. It sure is nice compared to bailing our water in a sinking ship in a storm, with no land in sight. Praise Jesus that is no longer the case.

If you know Jesus, I hope this energized you to look at your own journey with gratitude, and you have a refreshed spirit and excitement for what is to come. If you have not invited Jesus into your life, I ask that you start where I did—a heartfelt prayer for God to reveal Himself to you.

If you haven't accepted Jesus Christ in your life and you're ready, see appendix A (John 8:12). Thank you, Jesus, and thank you, Elizabeth, for loving this sinner so!

Appendix A

If you have made it here, the Holy Spirit may be convicting you that it is time to accept Jesus Christ as your Savior and Lord. I would highly suggest that after you have begun this work in your heart, you find a Christian you can share this desire with, one that is practicing their Christianity and an active member of their church. If you don't have that, find a local church, for they will be very welcoming to you, and if you don't feel that way, find another! There are plenty to choose from. Just ask if they practice Bible-based preaching, for that will help cut to the chase. Go sit in a couple of Sundays. Back row is just fine to start.

If the desire to accept Jesus Christ is immediate, you need to pray what is called a sinner's prayer. You can google that and find many examples. It should go something like this, "God, I know that I am a sinner and that I have been living my life without you. I want to change this and accept your forgiveness. I am ready to believe that Jesus Christ is the Son of God, that Jesus came to earth to suffer and die for all of our sins. Jesus bled for us all, died, and was buried. Jesus was resurrected from death and is now God. I am ready to accept Jesus Christ into my life and follow His teachings. I am ready to turn from my sins and desire a relationship with Jesus Christ as my Lord and Savior. I pray this in Jesus's name, amen."

Here is the bottom line. You're praying to acknowledge your sins, your desire to turn from them, and your desire to know Jesus Christ and invite Him into your heart.

Here is a scriptural-based way of looking at this using a tract called "Romans Road to Salvation."

1. "For all have sinned, and come short of the glory of God" (Romans 3:23).
2. "For the wages of sin is death; but the gift of God is eternal life through Jesus Christ our Lord" (Romans 6:23).
3. "But God demonstrates His own love toward us, in that while we were yet sinners, Christ dies for us" (Romans 5:8).
4. "That if you confess with your mouth Jesus as Lord, and believe in your heart that God raised Him from the dead, you will be saved; for with the heart a person believes, resulting in righteousness, and with the mouth he confesses, resulting in salvation" (Romans 10:9–10).
5. "For WHOEVER WILL CALL ON THE NAME OF THE LORD WILL BE SAVED" (Romans 10:13).

Keep moving forward. Let God show you when and where to look back!

About the Author

Benjamin Carter Jr. was born in Atlanta, Georgia, and grew up there. Growing up, Benjamin enjoyed outdoor activities. He loved to travel, hunt, fish, scuba dive, and later in life fly helicopters. Benjamin attended the College of Charleston with a major in business and loved being in a vibrant culture on the coast. Benjamin had always believed there was a God of some sort and always considered himself a spiritual person, but he did not always believe that Jesus was to be worshipped.

After several years in Benjamin's late twenties and early thirties of struggling with the consequences of alcohol, drugs, and unhealthy relationships, he found himself at a very scary bottom, with very real potential legal consequences. In 2015, Benjamin began a process of growth toward Jesus Christ that now finds him with a loving wife and two beautiful children. He is currently a seminary student at Southwestern Baptist Theological Seminary and a real estate agent selling land, living in Columbus, Georgia.

CPSIA information can be obtained
at www.ICGtesting.com
Printed in the USA
LVHW022304220621
690926LV00003B/83